CHIC
SIMPLE™

Components

"I give you the dreamy tunnels
midnight makes in our sleep...
I give you the lost map to my bed."

ANITA ENDREZZE

CHIC
SIMPLE ™
Components

B E D   L I N E N S

head to toe

ALFRED A. KNOPF   NEW YORK   1994

THIS IS A BORZOI BOOK
PUBLISHED BY ALFRED A. KNOPF, INC.

KIM JOHNSON GROSS   JEFF STONE

WRITTEN BY KATHRYN LIVINGSTON
PHOTOGRAPHS BY MARIA ROBLEDO
STYLED BY LYNN NIGRO

DESIGN AND ART DIRECTION
BY ROBERT VALENTINE INCORPORATED

ICON ILLUSTRATION BY ERIC HANSON

Library of Congress Cataloging-in-Publication Data
Gross, Kim Johnson.
Chic Simple. Bed Linens/Kim Johnson Gross, Jeff Stone, Kathryn Livingston.
p. cm.——(Chic Simple)
ISBN 0-679-43216-7
1. Bedding. I. Stone, Jeff. II. Livingston, Kathryn. III. Title. IV. Title: Bed Linens. V. Series.
TX315.G77 1994
643'.53–dc20
94-906
CIP

Grateful acknowledgment is made to the following for permission to
reprint previously published matierial:

Broken Moon Press: Excerpts from "I Give You" from *at the helm of twilight* by Anita Endrezze,
copyright © 1992 by Anita Endrezze (as reprinted in *Yellow Silk: Erotic Arts and Letters* edited
by Lily Pond and Richard Russo). Reprinted by permission of Broken Moon Press.

Vanity Fair: Excerpt from "A Lady and Her Court" by George Kalogerakis
(January, 1994), copyright © 1994 by The Conde Nast Publications Inc.
Reprinted by permission of *Vanity Fair.*

Printed in Canada
First Edition

CONTENTS

"The more you know, the less you need."

AUSTRALIAN ABORIGINAL SAYING

CHIC
SIMPLE ™

Chic Simple is a primer for living well but sensibly. It's for those who believe that quality of life does not come in accumulating things, but in paring down to the essentials. Chic Simple enables readers to bring value and style into their lives with economy and simplicity.

BED LINENS

A mountain of pillows, a sea of blankets, clouds of feather-filled duvets: things with which we spend one third of our lives. And sometimes more. For today's bedding is also a living space, an office, a cineplex. Sheets and shams, bedspread and bed skirt are props for our most personal environment: our private sanctuary. We retreat to a serious mattress to let muscles loose, stretch out the mind, and kick away the jagged edges of every day.

"Better wear out shoes than sheets."

ENGLISH PROVERB

THE HISTORY OF BED LINENS

ASSYRIANS, MEDES, AND PERSIANS, INSPIRED BY ANIMALS OF SYMBOLIC STRENGTH, SHAPED FRAMES OF METAL into lions, bulls, and serpents around piles of pelts, stacks of carpets, and, later, properly made-up woven bedclothes. A linen-dressed bed entombed in Egypt dates back to 3000 B.C. The Greek sleep was a silken affair with gilded purple coverlets and cushions at the head and feet. The Semite custom of reclining while eating and using the bed as banquet travelled to Roman Sybarites, who also laid the first double bed. By the Middle Ages, both Oriental and Occidental sleeping quarters evolved into cozy rooms within rooms, cloistered by four-posters, ample fabrics, and testers. The bed became social in the 17th century when the lavishly appointed ones were the focus of gatherings for the nobles of French court life. The bedroom as a private sanctum is a modern notion.

1 . *Power bed: The French "bed of justice." As long as the king was in Parliament, he reclined upon it, while the princess sat, the dukes stood, and all lesser officials knelt.* **2** . *Protest: John Lennon and Yoko Ono's week-long "Sleep-In" for peace at the Amsterdam Hilton.* **3** . *Vote-getter: Morning photo in Kennebunkport with Barbara and George Bush and all the grandchildren climbing into the family bed.*

"It was such a lovely day I thought it was a pity to get up."

SOMERSET MAUGHAM

FAMOUS BEDOPHILES

1 . *Oblomov, who never got up.* **2** . *Proust, who wrote his masterpiece* Remembrance of Things Past *between the sheets.* **3** . *Churchill, who strategized the fate of nations from his bed during World War II.* **4** . *Robert Rauschenberg, who tossed his pillow, sheet, and quilt onto his groundbreaking 1955 oil canvas* Bed. **5** . *Groucho Marx, who quipped: "Anything that can't be done in bed isn't worth doing at all."*

Tactile. "Gardens of the flesh" is how Cécile Sorel, the famous grande horizontale of the belle époque, referred to alluringly dressed beds. Just being near a nice bed we feel its ineluctable pull. Long before we climb into it, we have entered the realm of the senses. The invitation grows with the excitement of bedding a beloved. For centuries, European noblewomen preferred to sleep on shiny black satin to set off their skins and heighten their desirability. Today, we crave a richly nuanced interplay of textures from waffly piqués to fleecy wools, bubbly matelassés to plain smooth cotton percales, silky charmeuse to crisp linen damask.

STAIN FREE
Aquamirabilis is a massage oil that is relaxing for both body and mind since it won't leave a residue on your sheets.

MASSAGE
"To sleep: perchance to dream: Ay, there's the rub." According to Dr. Alan R. Hirsch, fruit can calm like a drug. "Fruit Hedonics" are the safest, sexiest mood-altering substances around. They have helped both insomniacs and anxiety sufferers.

Emotional. According to Dr. Spock, one out of every four of us was a Linus, sucking away at the same familiar, frayed corner of the satiny edging of a security blanket. In our beds we abandon our conscious to our subconscious and allow ourselves to dream. Beyond the edges of our bed lie the fascinating unknowns of those worlds Freud and Jung tried deciphering. When our external world becomes too fast-track, the bed is our safe harbor. To slide between freshly ironed linen is cool balm on a sweltering day. To curl into nappy flannels and a plump feather bed is to cocoon against winter's chills. We cry into our pillows and make hay under the covers. This is our ultimate comfort zone. We are brought back to that pivotal moment in childhood, when spanking clean from our bath we slipped into what we knew was a place of love and care—the very best place in the world.

BEDTIME STORIES

Fairy-tale Sleepers: Snow White, Goldilocks, The Frog Prince,
The Princess and the Pea, Little Red Riding Hood, Sleeping Beauty.

F O U N D A T I O N

Readied before birth, the nest and the cradle encapsulate life's central message: renewal. The cozy microcosms we build for safeguarding our young echo our own instinctive needs for nocturnal protection. Man started with beds of nature: a small depression in the ground, a hollowed-out tree trunk. For softness: a pile of leaves, a mat of reeds, a sack of straw. Ancient Germans slept in a shallow chest filled with moss. The Teutonic word for it was Bett.

> "It is a delicious moment, certainly, that of being nestled in bed and feeling that you shall drop gently to sleep."
>
> LEIGH HUNT

BOX SPRING AND BED SKIRT

MATTRESS WITH FITTED PAD

PILLOW, PILLOW PROTECTOR, AND
BUTTONED PILLOW SHAM

BEDSPREAD

FITTED BOTTOM SHEET

TOP SHEET, BLANKET, AND
BLANKET COVER

COMFORTER

THROW

The Mattress. A good foundation starts with an innerspring mattress and a box spring made with springs instead of a wood frame with foam. American mattresses are selling wider and thicker. California king (72" x 84") is usurping the classic king size (76" x 80"), while sales of queen size (60" x 80") mattresses are rivaling the old double (54" x 75"), also called full. Of the bed sizes that were standardized in the 1950s, the smallest is the twin (39" x 75"). But don't equate heft with luxury. It's the quality and density of materials used in the construction that makes the difference. Coil count is key. A full-size mattress should have at least 312 wire coils, a king at least 450. The wire in the coils should be no less than 13-gauge. The smaller the gauge, the sooner the beds wear out. There should be several layers of padding above and below the springs. The outside upholstery fabric covering is best when made of old-fashioned ticking: strong, closely woven, striped warp-faced fabrics. A mattress should last ten years. It should be six inches longer than the sleeper.

Feather Beds. Today's style of dressing the bed to satisfy our craving for all-natural layers has revived the feather bed. This mellow sack filled with down and feathers is the softest, warmest form of mattress padding and for most Americans is first encountered in European luxury hotels. A feather bed should be the exact size of the mattress. In the classic order the feather bed fits in between the mattress and bottom sheet. It is as close as one can get to sleeping on clouds.

STAYING WARM

To conserve the earth's energy resources and try to keep the planet free of unnecessary smoke, the hot water bottle is being rediscovered.

"Life is either always a tight-rope or a feather bed. Give me the tight-rope."

EDITH WHARTON

The Stuffing. Your main concern when it comes to feather beds and pillows is this: if you like sleeping on a cloud you must look into the silver lining. Information about the software inside is crucial to hygiene, allergies, upkeep, and simply getting your dollar's worth. The option for fillings is dizzying: down vs. feather, goose vs. duck, feather vs. fiberfill, nature's untreated cotton padding vs. technology's highly evolved microsynthetics. These days, for special reasons, bedding is also plumped with rare and luxurious particulars. Milkweed floss from Wales acts like a magnet to attract and hold irritating fine dander away from allergic addicts of down bedding. The best solution in natural fibers for those who are allergic, however, is silk filling from Italy, which adjusts its temperature to the body's needs. Cashmere is now also encased for its airy warmth. "Baffling" is the word not to be baffled by. It refers to the stitching that keeps the clusters of feathers and down—in unshifting "poufs"—to provide loft without lumps.

FRENCH, CONTINENTAL OR EUROSQUARE
(26" x 26")

KING
(26" x 36")

QUEEN
(26" x 30")

STANDARD
(20" x 26")

RUSSIAN
(14" x 14")

BOUDOIR OR BABY
(12" x 16")

NECK ROLL
(16" long;
6" diameter
sausage)

TRAVEL PILLOW
(20" x 15"
rolls up & ties into
compact bolster)

"Sleep is the best meditation."

DALAI LAMA

PILLOW POLICE

"Under penalty of law this tag may not be removed." What does it mean? This certificate of authenticity forces manufacturers to describe not only the exact content and properties of the materials but every chemical process the merchandise underwent. The Federal law was created in 1926. Don't worry, if you own the pillow you can remove the tags and sleep without fear.

Pillow Covers. It's pillows that largely define the bed's aesthetics and creature comforts. The pattern, texture, and border of pillows make for fantasy voyages to faraway places. They can evoke a French boudoir, Victorian England, or a bit of American country. Shams and Eurosquares—the decorative, bigger, envelope-style cases—draw the line between a masculine or feminine mood. When crisply piped or bordered with a flat flange, the look is more tailored and masculine. Hemmed in ruffles and lace, they are effectively feminine. Many women prefer to sleep on the small baby pillows—also convenient for taking on trips.

PILLOW TALKERS

CINEMATIC: 1. *Clark Gable and Claudette Colbert in* It Happened One Night 2. *Doris Day and Rock Hudson in* Pillow Talk 3. *Rex Harrison and Lilli Palmer in* The Fourposter 4. *Julie Christie and Donald Sutherland in* Don't Look Now EPIC: 1. *Othello and Desdemona* 2. *Samson and Delilah* ETHIC: 1. *The Prince of Conde and the Duke of Guise, conqueror and captive, shared a bed on the night of the Battle of Moncontour in 1569.* 2. *Mary Cunningham and William Agee, top execs at the Bendix Corporation*

Making it. During the Middle Ages "making a bed" was just that, filling a sack with straw at night and emptying it the next day. But bed making, following certain rules for a desired effect, was already in place among the ancient Persians. In the late Gothic period in northern Europe and England the linen fold was a favorite decorative motif applied to wainscots and screens. Later this evolved into the camp counselor's edict of the perfect hospital corner. The sheet had to be so tautly tucked, so precise that you could bounce a coin off it. These days when the fashion is to throw a duvet over all, the right system of making a bed eludes many people.

TURNING A CORNER

1. Place a flat sheet over mattress pad, letting it hang one foot beyond the head so it drapes evenly all around. 2. Make the first hospital corner by standing midway at the head of the bed. 3. Pick up a side hem and pull it toward you, lifting it to form a sharp triangular crease. 4. Use your other hand to smooth hanging part along the side of mattress and rounding corner. 5. Tautly tuck creased part over this and under the mattress. Repeat slant on other three corners.

S H E E T S

Hanging out newlyweds' stained bed sheets to air the morning after was part of the marriage ritual in many small villages from the Balkans to the Baltics. Sheets are the most private part of our beds. This is the zone of tenderness and love, snuggle and snore. Yet sheets have had many public uses: the togas of the ancients, the bandages of war, the white flag of surrender, the Ku Klux Klan's sheets of shame. Sheets lend themselves to infinite decorating touches. They can be made into curtains, slipcovers, wall coverings, and a spate of imaginative house embellishments.

> "His voice was as intimate as the rustle of sheets."
>
> DOROTHY PARKER

Cotton. It "breathes." It wicks body moisture away from the skin. It launders splendidly. And it gets better the more you use it. But its most endearing quality for the global generation is that it can look just as great and feel just as good when it is unironed. The cotton plant, gossypium, has had a greater impact on the economics and politics of the world than any other commodity. As "King Cotton" it controlled the American South—the cotton gin was the opening gun in the Industrial Revolution. This "royal plant" adapts itself to many homes. In the tropics it is a perennial 20-foot tree; in the U.S. it is a 4-foot annual shrub.

COTTON CLUB

Of the big four varieties, **SEA ISLAND** *wins for silkiness and refinement. It's grown exclusively in the West Indies and the islands off the Carolinas and Georgia coast.* **EGYPTIAN COTTON** *, which is also cultivated in America as well as the Sudan, is an extra-long lustrous staple.* **PIMA** *is a combination of the Braziliense and Barbadense strains. It is a fine, sturdy, extra-long staple with a slight brownish tint.* **AMERICAN UPLAND** *or hirsutum is cultivated throughout the U.S. cotton belt but a similar strain is grown in Malaysia, Peru, Burma, and Madagascar.*

Linen. The highest quality bed sheets are made of linen. They also are the most expensive. Linen's unequaled purity, gloss, and smoothness make it the healthiest material for sleeping. Spun and woven from flax, it has several advantages over cotton. Linen presents a less "woolly" surface, does not soil as readily, and does not retain moisture like the more "spongy" cotton. It comes in many weights from the heavy tarpaulin to the delicate handkerchief. Its cooling effect makes it ideal for summer. They grow softer and more precious with time and care. Two sets of fine linen sheets, in constant alternate use, can easily last a quarter century.

ORDER OF THE GARTER

Exquisite vintage linens unfortunately bear little resemblance to our modern standard bed sizes. Sheet suspenders glide and hide under the mattress and do the adjustment trick.

Antique Linens. A touch of Victoriana. Perhaps as an antidote to everything modern and machine-made, we find ourselves increasingly enamored of painstakingly handmade goods. Few of us own linen hand-me-downs but collecting vintage pieces at flea markets and consignment shops can be singularly satisfying, even affordable. Seasoned collectors will seek out damaged pieces and find creative ways to combine an exceptional embroidered corner or breathtaking old lace border with new materials. Don't try too hard to authenticate the French, Dutch, or Irish look of these homemade needleworks. Decorative motifs travelled fast from Transylvania to Pennsylvania. Even experts disagree on origins and signatures.

CARE AND FEEDING

Air and circulation in the linen closet is a must. Never wrap linen in plastic. It invites mildew. Beware of a cedar chest. It will discolor whites. If possible it is better to dry linens on the line than iron them. If you do iron, always do it while the linen is still slightly wet.

Blends. Just like clothes, bedclothes follow fashions. Ralph Lauren's cleverly staged ads, ablaze with atmosphere, are as artfully designed as the movie sets for the films of Bertolucci or Merchant Ivory. Color-coordinated bedding of boldly mixed patterns is a relatively recent phenomenon, since pure cotton and pure linen did not come in prints. It was not until the Americans wholeheartedly embraced the idea of "Drip Dry," "Wash and Wear," and "Easy Care" blends in the 1950s that the rich palettes of Wamsutta, Fieldcrest, and Springmaid entered the bedroom. "Designer Sheets"—coordinated soft goods with the signatures of American fashion-makers—were launched in the 1970s.

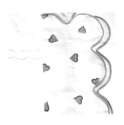

EUROPE'S CLASSICS

Porthault, in 1925, was the first to print patterns on the sheets. Porthault's signature heart linens touched the bodies of immortals Gary Cooper, Jacqueline Onassis, Tina Turner, and Woody Allen. Elizabeth Taylor, however, is a Pratesi aficionado along with the Pope, and many royals. Pratesi's trademark scallops on high thread-count linens are light as feathers, strong as steel.

Specialty Sheets. White satin was her second skin and Jean Harlow was at her sassiest on a tufted all-satin bed in *Dinner at Eight*. The male symbol of the Sexual Revolution, Hugh Hefner, slept in a round bed and Jayne Mansfield lolled on a pink silk heart-shaped bed. Did you ever wonder where they got their sheets? Actually, round-shaped or square-shaped, satin, flannel, or even wool and rubber or latex sheets are easy to obtain. They are found in linen departments, can be custom ordered, and are available through catalogues specializing in bed and bed dressing. You can indulge to your heart's delight, but get out your checkbook.

TOUCHING
TALES
For those so inclined:
FLANNEL: *soft*
SATIN: *sexy*
LATEX: *squeaky*

Simple Sheet. From swaddling to the shroud, the human drama starts and ends in simple white sheets. And when we come back to haunt our friends, we'll probably look like Casper. As our life goes on, our bedclothes enfold much of its meaning. We hide our nakedness and our naked truths under them: the insecurities of childhood, the passions of youth, the pains and pleasures of marriage and adult relationships. Here, we're visited by phantasmagoric nightmares and daydreams that spark inspired accomplishments. It is the place from which we first greet daylight and from which we say good night to the dark. And all in all—it's just a simple piece of cloth.

> "Ghosts wear bed sheets perfumed with our dreams."
>
> JOHN UPDIKE

BED COVERS

Today, we are keenly aware that beauty is as deep as its functional core. We crave design with as much substance as style. Paring away, we appreciate the value of basics. What does it take to feel perfectly covered for a good night's rest? For some, nothing surpasses a crisp white sheet and a warm blanket.

"Life is something to do when you can't get to sleep."

FRAN LEBOWITZ

Blankets. The light embrace of a silken duvet is different from the firm hug of a tightly tucked blanket. America's blanket history is entwined with the Hudson's Bay Company, whose royal charter was granted in 1670 to establish English contact with the Indian nations of America's interior. To this day, woven in England of the finest virgin wool, the creamy Hudson's Bay "Point Blanket" is identical to those traded for pelts. In the West, Pendleton blankets copied the tribal totems, the Nez Percé's arrowhead or the Navajo's thunderbolt, in the clear cool colors of the Pacific Northwest. A reminder of when bed was a saddle by the fire under an open sky.

NEW AGE
Thermarest and Polartech. Manmade water-repellent fleeces are the new wool, soft, strong, and warm.

HUDSON'S BAY
Indigo markings, or points, stand for the number of skins exchanged for it by Native Americans.

Comforters. Comforter or duvet, what is the difference? A duvet is actually a down- or feather-filled comforter. Lightweight and almost dust-free, its self-adjusting warmth means no other blankets are needed; bed making becomes a cinch. The highest quality duvet is filled with white goose down from Hungary. "Down and feathers" is finer than "feather and down." Air them regularly. Dry clean only. Keep them fresh with duvet covers or top sheets or old-fashioned European comforter covers that frame the silken tufting of more formal comforters. Use them in place of a bedspread on top of the blanket liner.

SNUGGLING
The Middle Ages lay dark in feather-warmed communal huddles. Only nightcaps were worn. Everyone was naked. The shared goal was to keep out drafts.

BUNDLING
Courting one's beloved in bed was a custom in 18th-century America. Lovers would be allowed to lie fully clothed next to each other with a wooden plank placed between them.

BAFFLING
Baffling is the stitching that keeps the loft distributed within the proper cubic inches or clusters.

Quilts. When the early settlers came to the New World, they brought with them their European layered coverlets. Of course, fabric was unavailable in the new country, so the women kept patching new pieces of torn garment fabrics to the parts where the coverlet began to fray. American quilts are usually made of cotton but filling is sometimes wool. There are three layers: top design, the batting or lining, and the backing. Popular patchwork patterns are the "Double-Wedding Ring," "Flying Geese," "The Sunflower," and "The Drunkard's Path," which was created during the Temperance Movement. Quilts, whether as spread, bed cover, throw, or wall hanging, epitomize the American tenet that useful is beautiful.

"The quilt is where the desire for beauty and the moral scorn for extravagance used to intersect."

ROBERT HUGHES

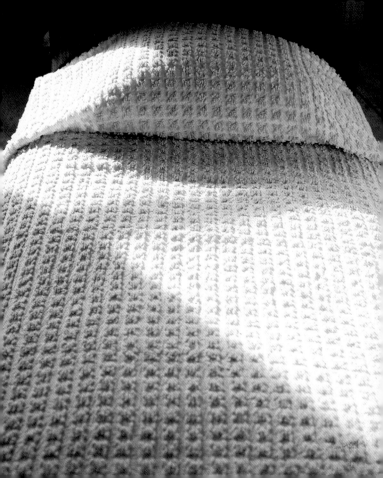

Bedspread. The French *lit en baldaquin* travelled to the Colonies as the canopy bed and that great extravaganza, the *lit à couronne* with its shower of fabric spilling down from the ceiling and matching bedspread, made a big re-entry in the conspicuously expensive bedrooms of the Eighties. Now the bedspread is on the wane. Many people find a pretty blanket cover will do just as well. The new-generation spreads tend to be lighter coverlets of washable piqué or embossed cotton. Chenille of the Forties and Fifties is emerging as the comeback kid. Timeless and nostalgic, it is as hip as it is easy to keep fresh.

THE SPREAD IS
NOT DEAD

Established by the American upper class and their servants, the proper bed is still structured with these must ingredients: the blanket cover and the quilted bedspread, which hide all the bedclothes during the day. The blanket cover ranges from seersucker to luxurious French textile and is to the blanket what a pillow protector is to a pillow.

M I X I N G

Like all highly evolved household species, the bed is a complex composite of the predictable and capricious. Today's bed style is torn between two directional urges. One is the dress-it-down, "deconstructed" route: a romance of wrinkles. Fresh-as-a-daisy but lived-in, natural, organic, undyed, unbleached, sun-bleached, a plumped-up nest of eco-conscious earthly delights. The other follows a more exhibitionistic impulse: the bed as a theater. A stage set for free-wheeling self-expression, cross-cultural experimentation, layers as thick as stage makeup. A dream trip.

> "I honestly believe there is absolutely nothing like going to bed with a good book. Or a friend who's read one."
>
> PHYLLIS DILLER

ADDING ON

*Taking the black and white geometry to new dimensions: A whole new grouping
but all in the same color family. New shapes and sizes added. A checkered pillow.
A quilted cover on the headboard.*

MORE DRAMA

Here color makes a splash. Red adds flamboyance. The original black and white graphics easily take on other bold patterns—paisleys, plaids, stripes, animal prints.

Layering. It used to be design anathema to go beyond three color families in mixing florals and solids, checks and stripes to create a bedroom and stay this side of overload. Now we think nothing of tossing in as many as a dozen fabrics to create a look. Our late-twentieth-century sensibilities have been expanded by travel. Our personal image banks are stacked with deep-toned, exotic fabrics, elegant mixes of textures, shapes, and graphics that evoke other places, other periods, and resonate with the tribal beats of the global village.

Throws. The very word is imbued with spontaneity and serendipity. Throws have two functions: to yield extra warmth on the coldest nights or to add panache to the look of the bedroom. They are usually rolled up at the foot of the bed. Sometimes they move off the bed to lend style to a nearby easy chair, or a chest. They can be as light as a veil of mosquito netting swathed around a bed's iron frame or as heavy as a Kilim rug and a thick afghan crocheted in Belarus. Today's favorites are rich paisleys or airy knitted wisps.

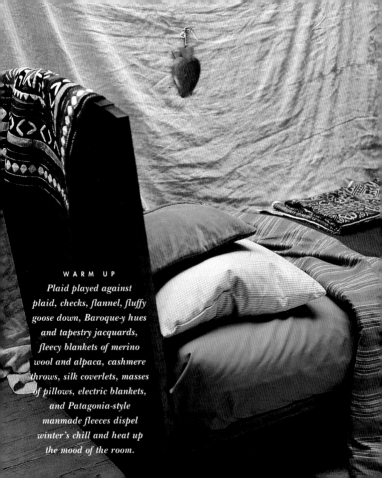

WARM UP

Plaid played against plaid, checks, flannel, fluffy goose down, Baroque-y hues and tapestry jacquards, fleecy blankets of merino wool and alpaca, cashmere throws, silk coverlets, masses of pillows, electric blankets, and Patagonia-style manmade fleeces dispel winter's chill and heat up the mood of the room.

COOL DOWN

*Crisp white polka dots
embroidered white-on-white,
frosty white piqué, gauzy
antique chambray and
dimity, jerusaic lace from
Venice, puckered gingham,
scaled-down English roses,
graceful French carnation
prints, airy knits, and breeze-
dried percale are summer
soothers.*

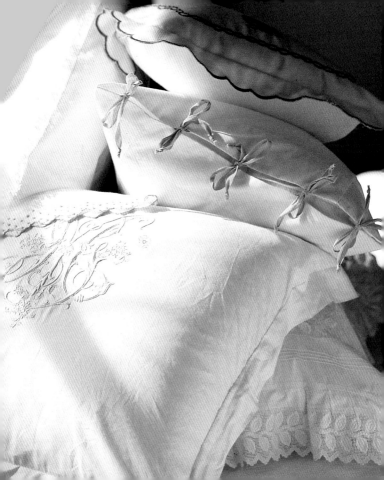

Details. While she was in prison, Madame Mao is said to have kept busy embroidering, secretly signing the character of her name into handkerchief corners. Some catalogues and department stores still refer to bed linens as domestics, because until recently, bedding was made by loving hands at home. Entire lifetimes of women were consumed with cutting and hemming wide bolts of fabric, painstakingly embroidering, appliquéing, crocheting, and quilting bedding that would be passed down through the generations. Their legacy continues with eyelets, smocking, faggoting, hemstitching, and scalloping still popular today.

MONOGRAM SUBSTITUTES
For Vanderbilts, Astors, and Rockefellers, the monograms used to cost more than the sheets. Now more outrageous signatures are possible: a heartful of condoms on the safe side, or a heartfelt tattoo for a dangerous lover.

Nerve Center. The bed is now a lot more than sleep space. It can serve as an unofficial office, an entertainment complex, a breakfast perch, headquarters for social networking, a platform where the whole family can gather. Don't fight maximizing the bed's use. This nestling nook of pillows and blankets is really more like a living room or a library today. Think of it as an open loft where function

is no longer compartmentalized but shifts into service zones, dissolves into vignettes of different facets of life depending on the hour or the lighting. Armed with a laptop, rolodex, filofax, or a video remote, this need not be a preserve of passive activity at all. Swoop up the bedding from a daybed or roll away the Murphy bed and the freed space offers options having nothing to do with privacy or sleep.

GLOBAL ROMANCE

Cosmic and meditative vibes.
Echoes of winds whistling
through Mexican pyramids
reclaimed by jungle. Ricocheting
Indonesian ceremonial secrets.
Sounds of silence in the ancient
canyons of the earth-
worshipping, mesa-dwelling
Anasazi.

Romantic. Among the world's most photographed beds are Lord Neidpath's twin Chinese Chippendale daybeds in the drawing room at Stanway in Gloucestershire, England. Mick Jagger, David Bowie, and Christy Turlington are some of the celebrities who have been snapped romping under their witty jade pagoda tops. In spite of the grandeur of these silk-cushioned daybeds they infuse the room with a certain playfulness. Romance is seldom formal. Nor need the romantic bedroom be a wallow in Victorian ribbons and lace. The offhand mixes are perhaps a more potent seduction.

WOMEN IN BED 1. *Marilyn Monroe, when asked what she had on in bed: "Some Arpège and Bartók on the radio." 2. Coco Chanel, the fashion label of the century, reminded herself nightly that she was a working girl. In stark contrast to her luxuriously decorated maison of couture, she slept across the street in the simplest bed of a servant's room on the top floor of The Ritz. 3. Buck Henry: "Men should never make passes at women who wear sheets." 4. Brooke Shields: "What does 'good in bed' mean to me? When I'm sick and stay home from school propped up with lots of pillows watching TV and my mom brings me soup."*

"All sensuality is one, though it takes many forms, as all purity is one."

HENRY DAVID THOREAU

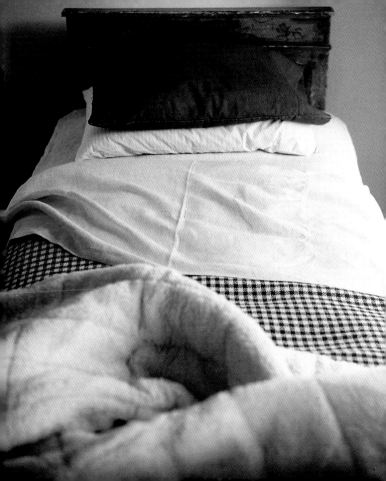

Rugged Romance. Imagine a wind-whipped, snow-covered hut. Two people in a smallish bed on a cold winter night. Snow falling. A candle flickering in the corner. Two people alone, far from everything and everyone. Cuddling in a cocoon of checks and plaids. Wild West denim, a wonderful warm blanket from Scotland, flannel, homespun throws, Nordic feathers filling fluffy headrests.

"When the guns begin they think of firelit homes, clean beds, and wives."

SIEGFRIED SASSOON *Soldiers Are Dreamers*

"It is the beholder who lends to the beautiful thing its myriad meanings and sets it in some relation to the age." OSCAR WILDE

Staging. The theater of the bed: the province of our love and dreams—our most private moments—has become a sort of public proscenium, where we reveal our personalized interpretation of comfort. Imagination is the only limit. Don't be intimidated: if you use enough brazen patterns they neutralize each other. Every texture can be made to work together. Discerning individualists now seldom buy completely matched sets for the bed, just as they no longer are dressed by one designer. Start in with some of your favorite things: a treasured vintage linen spread, a pillow sham made from a favorite flannel shirt —it's your stage.

BASIC WARDROBE

"When I made bed linens, what I simply did is what I try to do with my clothes: form a wardrobe of linens. One set of sheets would go with another and you could keep adding to your collection. Every now and then, you could engage in something not so practical—just like a foolish accessory. And I preferred to work with neutrals. For me, the bed should always be inviting: it should help induce sleep and not-too-quick an awakening which you might get with too strong a color or too strong a design."

GEOFFREY BEENE

Simple Bed. At the end of the twentieth century we have redefined what's vital to our comfort and contentment. In a world of limited space and time it is both a surprise and a relief how little we need for a good sleep. Combing cultures we recognize the space-saving wisdom of the Japanese sleep, which was traditionally on the floor between two quilts. Each morning the shiki-futon, or underquilt, and the kake-futon, or overquilt, were rolled up, put in the closet, and the room was used for dining. Similarly, our attitude to covering has changed. The European way of sleeping year-round under a light, temperature-adjusting down comforter appeals to our sense of stripped-down luxury. All those layers—top sheet, blanket, bedspread, and throw are nice, but all we really need is a cotton-padded futon, a bottom sheet, a duvet, and a pillow. It's in sync with the eco-sensitive rule: reduce, reuse, recycle. What's more, this kind of bedding demands less effort. The secret of its serene elegance is that its form is function.

 # first aid.

An underlying philosophy of the late 20th century is that quality is less about status and more about personal pleasure, through fine materials and good craftsmanship—objects which, with proper care, actually improve with time. This is particularly true of bedding, whether the materials come from nature, whether they're synthetic or blends. The Federal Trade Commission law requires U.S. manufacturers to attach labels to most white goods. Tags on sheets, blankets, and pillows explain exact fiber content and suggest ways to keep them clean.

LOFT HIERARCHY

Optimal thermal properties and maximum comfort in pillows and comforter come from large European white goose down clusters. Baffle construction—or box stitching in comforters—increases their longevity. The ultimate pillow is 650 fill power Hungarian goose down covered with 250 to 300 thread cotton damask ticking.

Goose down is finer than duck down. Down is finer than feathers. Feathers must be enclosed in tightly-woven ticking so they won't pierce through their coverings. Fiberfill and microsynthetics are recommended for those allergic to feathers, but certain synthetics develop a rubbery odor after a while. Today, down insulators are often combined with white milkweed floss to provide hypo-allergenic bedding solutions. For example, 70 percent white goose down with 30 percent white milkweed floss feels exceptionally luxurious and is tolerable by many allergy sufferers. The alternatives are non-down-filled comforters with box-stitched cotton, silk, or cashmere fillings.

THREAD COUNT

The higher the thread count, the finer the quality of the sheet. Superb Egyptian cotton has a total number of 350 threads per square inch. The standard American 200 to 250 thread sheet is good, strong, and beautiful.

DENIER

Denier is a unit of weight for threads of silk, rayon, or nylon, equal to .05 grams per 450 meters. The lower the denier number, the higher the quality of the fabric.

TICKING TIME

Old-fashioned Bohemia ticking in closely-woven satin and twill with colored warp stripes and jacquard panels in various weights are far superior to sateens or drills that usually have floral designs and back-filled finishes to fill up the interstices of their lower thread counts.

MADE TO ORDER

For the eco-nervous, for those allergic to man-made fibers or to horsehair, pig's hair, etc., or just the opposite, for those who long for an almost anachronistic but purist all-horsehair mattress, and, finally, for those with difficult-to-fit antique beds—there is the custom mattress and also the custom box spring. Antique dealers can usually recommend a nearby specialist for custom sizes.

In Connecticut, the Norwalk Mattress Company charges between $400 and $1,700 for custom-shaped mattresses filled with natural layers: burlap, horsehair, cotton felt, upholstered with cotton ticking. The Allergy Relief Shop in Knoxville, Tennessee, goes beyond mattresses to create bedding free of all chemical urethane foam lining, which may make commercial mattresses more durable, comfortable, and flame retardant but which can be major irritants to the allergy-prone. Their sheets, mattresses, mattress covers, and bed coverings are made of organic cotton. Their innerspring mattresses are thicker than most commercial mattresses, with layers of pure cotton to a depth of nine inches. Their box springs avoid wood, as some people are unaware of their allergies to certain types of wood.

Warning: Never use while sleeping.
WARNING WITH A HAIR DRIER,
cited in U.S. News and World Report

The ultimate horsehair-mattress maker is Charles H. Beckley of New York. While some of the finest horsehair is indeed made entirely of the long-plaited tails of Argentine stallions, cut and spun, it is a mistaken notion that horses are shaved to obtain their hair. And not all horsehair comes from the tail. But the hair from the tail has the most pleasant crunch and provides the most comfort. It is also the most costly. A queen-size all-horsehair mattress costs $2,400. The Beckley Company also makes part-horsehair mattresses, which are half-filled with blended cotton felt and loose horsehair and crowned at the center to seven inches for more even wear and, therefore, there is a special Beckley box spring. It features eight-way hand-tied coils, covered with a layer each of burlap, cotton felt, and cotton ticking. Most custom mattress houses also take orders for round, heart-shaped, or other custom mattresses, and box springs as well.

The company that supplies the British Royal Family's mattresses, Heals of London, is famous for its awesome coil-count mattresses. Through ABC Carpet & Home in New York, these special mattresses—Kilcaire, Hanley, and Lingfield—are now available to Americans for a cost of $3,995 to $9,995. They feature teased-out hair from cattle and horses "of the highest quality." The wool filler comes from Sussex sheep and the springs, tucked into Hessian pockets, are "star-lashed" with eight knots for polished flax cord.

VILE BEDFELLOWS

An environmental architectural firm in Connecticut has called the insides of many a modern mattress a "toxic waste dump." Urethane foam lining can produce fumes, synthetic coverings contain V.O.C.'s or volatile organic compounds like formaldehyde. Upholstery, batting, and foam are often treated with flame retardants, mildew-preventing biocides, and chemical-emitting stain guards.

MATTRESS PADDING

Horsehair, pig's hair, sisal, coconut fibers, burlap, untreated cotton, foam, fiberfill—all in many layers. The more layers on both sides of the coiled springs, the finer the mattress. The mattress cover itself is easiest to keep fresh when cotton-filled and baffle-stitched.

> "When I was a child what I wanted to be when I grew up was an invalid."

QUENTIN CRISP

The Naked Civil Servant

MATTRESS PADDING ALTERNATIVES

The feather bed is only one form of mattress padding. For bed-wetting infants and aging incontinents there are rubberized sheets, soft and nappy but impermeable. They should be the exact size of the mattress top and smoothed between mattress cover and bottom sheet.

MATTRESS ALTERNATIVES

About 15 percent of Americans sleep on water beds, a concept launched in 1967 but borrowed from Persian nomads who slept on water-filled goatskins three thousand years ago. Futons from Japan, hammocks from the Yucatan, and sleeping bags are gaining ground with the rest of the population.

SUSPICIOUS STAINS

Remember, those "damned spots" must be removed as quickly as possible! Wine: white will come out with hot soapy washing; red wine stains must be sprinkled with salt and then dropped into cold water. Saturate with club soda or baking soda if stubborn. Scorch marks or rust or mildew: apply a paste of salt mixed with lemon juice, rinse right away, wash in borax solution. Blood: use only cold water; hot water will set the stain. Candle wax: harden with an ice cube, then flake away, place between brown paper and iron with a warm iron so paper absorbs wax. Semen: detergent and washing machine. Grease: sprinkle baking soda and leave on for a few hours.

ANTIQUE LINEN & LACE

All lace coverings and thin fabrics such as muslin should be shaken free of dust before washing in gentle warm suds. Always remove your hand jewelry so it won't snag these delicate old pieces if you wash them by hand. A dingy bit of lace can use extra soaking. Starch, if it is to be applied, should be light and done while the delicate fabrics are still wet. Lace and crochet-work should be pinned on sheets with non-rusting pins.

> ## "It is difficult to see why lace should be so expensive; it is mostly holes."
>
> ### MARY WILSON LITTLE

Pin corners first. Always press lace along the lengthwise threads. Iron linen always on the straight and never on the bias. This will help prevent rippling and puckering. Gently press richly ornate embroidered pieces of linen on a fluffy towel with the raised side face down on the padded surface. They should still be damp. The iron should be only medium hot. "A stitch in time saves nine" goes the old homily. Mending is an important aspect of keeping and restoring vintage linen.

Professionals can often make repairs that are invisible. If you discover a tear before washing an antique item, it is better to mend or at least secure the part before laundering. Valuable antiques should be turned over to professionals for darning and patching. If you splurge on a museum-quality piece, have a professional clean it. Read: Potions from the Baptist Church in Kentucky *and* The Linen Closet *by Michele Durkson Clise. Final Hint from Heloise: "After textiles soak for 14 minutes, the dirt is loose. After that the dirt in the water starts soaking back into the fabric."*

WASHING WOOLS

Always check labels. Some wool blankets and throws with airy weaves should never be washed, for the pattern itself may be permanently altered. Chlorine bleach will damage most wool fibers. Dry clean cashmere, afghans, tapestry weaves, and paisley throws.

> "Too soft a bed tends to make people dream which is unhealthy and weakening."
>
> *How Girls Can Help Their Country,*
> *Girl Scout Manual, 1913*

TABLE TO BED

Designer Betsey Johnson, a longtime collector of antique bedding, found that old tablecloths made better bedspreads than old bedspreads. "The lacework, the appliqué, the inlay survived better and the huge old tables were more like the sizes of modern beds."

ABOUT FINISH

Mercerized means that yarn has been given extra strength to be receptive to color. Mercerized dyed cotton has a certain luster.

Sanforized means that the fabric was preshrunk, and its size will not be affected by laundering.

Durable Press makes a fabric less susceptible to wrinkling and usually needs little or no ironing.

300 THREAD JUNIORS

Frette has seduced many with their 300 thread, 100 percent Egyptian cotton sheets. With each washing they improve and consequently are a worthy investment, but investment is the qualifying word. For those of us that find the initial down payment too dear, Frette has come out with a luxury diffusion line of 200 thread count at half the price.

ADJUSTING TO FOREIGN SIZING

While American and many European mattress sizes conform, bed linens will vary in size from one manufacturer to the next and from one country to the next. U.S. standard sizes apply to sheets and pillowcases made by large manufacturers. Here are some helpful hints:

1. *Flat sheets should be at least twenty-four inches wider and longer than the mattress.*
2. *European fitted sheets may need a "box" to deepen the standard U.S. mattress, which is 6" to 8" deep.*
3. *Comforter—or duvet—covers should be the same sizes as the comforter.*
4. *Pillowcases should be at least four inches longer than the pillow.*

U.S. STANDARD VS. EUROPEAN SIZING (IN WHITE)

	Twin/Single	Full/Double	Queen	King	Calif. King
Mattress	*39" x 75"*	*54" x 75"*	*60" x 80"*	*76" x 80"*	*72" x 84"*
	90cm x 190cm (35" x 75")	*135cm x 190cm (53" x 75")*	*150cm x 200cm (59" x 79")*	*180cm x 200cm (71" x 79")*	
Flat Sheet	*66" x 96"*	*81" x 96"*	*90" x 102"*	*108" x 102"*	*108" x 102"*
	180cm x 260cm (71" x 102")	*230cm x 260cm (91" x 102")*	*208cm x 300cm (90" x 118")*	*270cm x 300cm (106" x 118")*	
Pillow	*20" x 26"*	*20" x 26"*	*20" x 30"*	*20" x 36"*	*20" x 36"*
	50cm x 75cm (20" x 30")	*50cm x 75cm (20" x 30")*	*50cm x 90cm (20" x 35")*	*50cm x 90cm (20" x 35")*	
Pillowcase	*20" x 30"*	*20" x 30"*	*20" x 34"*	*20" x 40"*	*20" x 40"*
	50cm x 90cm (20" x 35")	*50cm x 90cm (20" x 35")*	*50 cm x 105cm (20" x 40")*	*50cm x 105cm (20" x 40")*	
Comforter/ Duvet and Cover	*68" x 86"*	*76" x 86"*	*86" x 86"*	*100" x 90"*	*100" x 90"*
	135cm x 220cm (53" x 87")	*200cm x 220cm (79" x 87")*	*230cm x 220cm (91" x 87")*	*260cm x 220cm (102" x 87")*	

CLEAN PILLOWS

Washing and dry cleaning of pillows, whether filled with down, polyester, foam rubber, cotton, or silk, is to be avoided. This is why pillow protectors are so important. These zippered protectors should be washed frequently and the pillows themselves should be aired regularly to keep them fresh. However, if they must be washed, the following advice comes from one of the foremost experts in refurbishing valuable bedding and antique linens, Elisabetta Anichini of Fine Linen Care at 268 Henry Street, Brooklyn Heights, New York, 11201, phone (718) 834-0466.

"A down pillow should be washed in a dry manner, as in dry cleaning, or in a washing machine with light biodegradable soap. If the fragrance is too strong from the dry cleaning chemicals, which is usually the case, the pillow becomes less pleasurable. I always prefer natural ingredients for the care of fine linens—soda or vinegar versus bleach for example. Many decorative pillows contain some unnatural substances, such as foam rubber. These could be removed prior to washing by unstitching part of the pillow.

"When laundering down pillows, it is not the washing but the drying process that becomes critical. Never put a down pillow in a dryer but hang it outside. Shake it several times during the day, maybe as often as once every hour, this way and that, so the down feathers inside don't stick together and form unbalanced clumps. Always check the casing before washing. The absolute horror would be a weak case with all the feathers bursting out during the wash or during this shaking and moving process."

BETWEEN THE SHEETS

The name of a cocktail at New York's Rainbow Room. **The recipe:** Mix one jigger of brandy, one jigger of Cointreau, one jigger of Benedictine, and the juice of one lemon. Sugar to taste. Shake with crushed ice in a cocktail shaker. Pour into cocktail glass.

"Only sleep on white sheets—anything else would change your personality."

KATHARINE HEPBURN

where. A Chic Simple store looks

out on the world beyond its shopwindow. Items are practical and

comfortable and will work with pieces bought elsewhere. The

store can be a cottage industry or a global chain, but even with an

international vision it is still rooted in tradition, quality, and value.

FREEDOM OF CHOICE

Even as the world shrinks and chain stores expand globally, there are plenty of locales where choice is limited if there is any choice at all. However, most manufacturers today can aid you in finding a store or even mail direct to you. The U.S. numbers listed below will help give you freedom of choice.

DESIGNERS AND DISTRIBUTORS

Anichini 800/553-5309
Garnet Hill 800/622-6216
Wamsutta 800/344-2142
Palais Royal 800/322-3911

Ralph Lauren 800/775-7656
Porthault 212/688-1660
Pratesi 212/288-2315

United States

CALIFORNIA

EAST MEETS WEST
658 North Larchmont
Boulevard
Hollywood, CA 90004
213/461-1389
(Antique quilts and Americana)

ROOM WITH A VIEW
1600 Montana Avenue
Santa Monica, CA 90403
310/998-5858
(Bed linens)

SCHEUER LINENS
318 Stockton Street
San Francisco, CA 94108
415/392-2813
(European linens)

SUE FISHER KING
3067 Sacramento Street
San Francisco, CA 94115
415/922-7276
(Imported bed linens)

CONNECTICUT

DUXIANA
15 West Putnam Avenue
Greenwich, CT 06830
203/661-7162 or
800/382-6662
(European bed linens,
Swedish dux mattresses)

NORWALK MATTRESS
COMPANY
145 West Cedar Street
Norwalk, CT 06854
203/866-6913
(Mattresses in custom sizes)

FLORIDA

LETA AUSTIN FOSTER
205 Phipps Plaza
Palm Beach, FL 33480
407/655-5489
(Bed linens)

METTLER'S
35 South Boulevard of
Presidents
Sarasota, FL 34236
813/338-3991
(Bed linens)

GEORGIA

RICH'S
Lenox Square Shopping
Mall
3393 Peachtree Road
Atlanta, GA 30326
404/231-2611

HAWAII

LIBERTY HOUSE
Ala Moana
Waikiki Beach
Honolulu, HI 96845
808/941-2345
(Bed linens and bedding)

ILLINOIS

ARRELLE FINE LINENS
445 North Wells Street
Chicago, IL 60610
312/321-3696
(Egyptian cotton sheets)

MASSACHUSETTS

LOUIS, BOSTON
234 Berkeley Street
Boston, MA 02116
617/262-6100 or
800/225-5135
(Bed linens)

NEW HAMPSHIRE

ANICHINI OUTLET
STORE
Powerhouse Mall
West Lebanon, NH 03784
603/298-8656
(Discontinued and over-
stocked Anichini linens at
reduced prices)

EASTERN MOUNTAIN
SPORTS
1 Vose Farm Road
Peterborough, NH 03458
603/924-9571
*(Down and synthetic sleeping
bags)*

NEW JERSEY

HAMILTON ADAMS
IMPORTS LTD.
P.O. Box 2489
101 County Avenue
Secaucus, NJ 07096-2489
201/866-3250
(Bed linens)

NEW MEXICO

FAIRCLOTH
228 Old Santa Fe Trail
Santa Fe, NM 87501
505/982-8700
(Antique bed linens)

NEW YORK

JUDI BOISSON
AMERICAN COUNTRY
96 Main Street
Southampton, NY 11968
516/283-5466
(Quilts, bed linens)

New York City

ABC CARPET & HOME
888 Broadway
New York, NY 10003
212/473-3000
*(Bed accessories, contemporary
furnishings, and linens)*

AD HOC SOFTWARES
410 West Broadway
New York, NY 10012
212/925-2652
(Bed linens, home accessories)

ALICE'S ANTIQUES
505 Columbus Avenue
New York, NY 10024
212/874-3400

ANGEL ZIMICK
represented by
Metropolitan Design Group
80 West 40th Street
New York, NY 10018
212/944-6110
*(Designer of fine linens for the
bed and home)*

ARCHIPELAGO
Available at Barneys, Ad
Hoc, and Takashimaya
*(Fine linens for the home,
decorative pillows)*

BERGDORF GOODMAN
754 Fifth Avenue
New York, NY 10019
212/753-7300
(Bed linens)

BOCA GRANDE
89 Spring Street
New York, NY 10012
212/966-7716
(Imported bedding)

CHARLES BECKLEY
306 East 61st Street,
New York, NY 10021
212/759-8450
*(Specializing in high-quality
horsehair mattresses)*

DAVID FORSTER &
COMPANY
35 West 57th Street
New York, NY 10019
212/753-9096
(Custom linens for any size)

DESCAMPS
723 Madison Avenue
New York, NY 10021
212/355-2522
(Imported French linens)

DIAL-A-MATTRESS
31-10 48th Avenue
Long Island City, NY 11101
800/MATTRES
*(Bedding and bedding-related
products)*

THE DOWN COMPANY
880 Madison Avenue
New York, NY 10021
212/517-3696
(Down comforters, pillows)

DOWN QUILT SHOP
518 Columbus Avenue
New York, NY 10024
212/496-8980
*(Bedding, patchwork quilts,
and down comforters)*

E. BRAUN & CO.
717 Madison Avenue
New York, NY 10021
212/838-0650
*(Linens in silk, linen, cotton,
and cotton blends with custom
embellishments)*

ELDRIDGE TEXTILE
COMPANY
277 Grand Street
New York, NY 10002
212/925-1523
(Linens)

FRETTE LINEN
799 Madison Avenue
New York, NY 10021
212/988-5221
(Fine Italian bed linens)

HENRO
525 Broome Street
New York, NY 10013
212/343-0221
(Vintage bed linens)

KALEIDOSCOPE
365 Canal Street
New York, NY 10013
212/274-8006
(Tattoo design, pillows, etc.)

KELTER-MALCÉ
361 Bleecker Street
New York, NY 10014
212/989-6760
*(Quilts, antique ticking
fabric, homespun linen)*

J. SCHACHTER
5 Cook Street
Brooklyn, NY 11206
718/384-2100 or
800/468-6233
(Custom and ready-made)

LÉRON LINENS
750 Madison Avenue
New York, NY 10021
212/249-3188 or
212/753-6700
*(Elaborate embroidery and
appliqué work; also will
design linens to match
wallpaper or fabric of choice)*

MIKE AND MISHA
PILLOW & QUILTS INC.
114-16 First Street
New York, NY 10009
212/260-7270
(Down and feather quilts)

THE NOOSE
261 West 19th Street
New York, NY 10011
212/807-1789
(Exotic, adventurous bedding)

PORTHAULT
18 East 69th Street
New York, NY 10021
212/688-1660
(French bed linens)
Catalogue available

PORTICO BED & BATH
139 Spring Street
New York, NY 10012
212/941-7722
*(Bed and bath linens, home
accessories)*

PRATESI
829 Madison Avenue
New York, NY 10021
212/288-2315
(Italian bed linens)

SUSAN PARRISH
ANTIQUES
390 Bleecker Street
New York, NY 10014
212/645-5020
*(Antique American textiles,
quilts, trade blankets, Navajo
weavings, vintage linens,
coverlets, and bedding)*

TAKASHIMAYA
693 Fifth Avenue
New York, NY 10022
212/350-0100
*(Japanese department store,
bed linens)*

TERRA VERDE
120 Wooster Street
New York, NY 10012
212/925-4533

THOS. K. WOODARD
AMERICAN ANTIQUES &
QUILTS
799 Madison Avenue
New York, NY 10021
212/988-2906
(American antique quilts)

WOLFMAN • GOLD &
GOOD CO.
116 Greene Street
New York, NY 10012
212/431-1888
(Bed linens)

ZONA
97 Greene Street
New York, NY 10012
212/925-6750
(Bedroom accessories)

TENNESSEE

THE ALLERGY RELIEF
SHOP
3371 Whittle Springs Road
Knoxville, TN 37917
615/522-2795 or
800/626-2810
*(Custom-made bedding free of
allergy-causing substances)*

BELLA LINEA
NASHVILLE
Patdock Place
73 Whitebridge Road 104
Nashville, TN 37205
615/352-4041

TEXAS

MES AMIS
1749 Post Oak Boulevard
Houston, TX 77056
713/840-8795
(Bed linens)

NUVO
3900 Cedar Springs
Dallas, TX 75219
214/522-6891
(Bed linens)

STANLEY KORSHAK
500 Crescent Court,
Suite 100
Dallas, TX 75201
214/871-3600
(Bed linens)

TOKERUD AND CO.
4606 Greenbrier
Houston, TX 77005-1524
713/520-8666
(Bed linens)

VERMONT

ANICHINI
Route 110
Turnbridge, VT 05077
800/533-5309
*(Fine imported linens and
textiles from Italy)*

POLO/RALPH LAUREN
FACTORY STORE
Routes 11 and 30
Manchester, VT 05255
802/362-2340
*(Bed linens and bedding
accessories)*

WASHINGTON

INSIDE
1305 First Avenue
Seattle, WA 98101
206/623-5646
(Bed linens)

R.H. MACY & CO., INC.
(Bullock's, I. Magnin,
Aéropostale)
Macy's Herald Square
151 West 34th Street
New York, NY 10001
800/45-MACYS
212/695-4400 for East Coast
listings, 415/954-6000 for
West Coast listings
(Bed linens and accessories)

WAMSUTTA
1285 Avenue of the
Americas
New York, NY 10019
800/344-2142
(Bed linens)

WEST POINT STEVENS
P.O. Box 609
West Point, GA 31833
800/533-8229
(Bed linens and accessories)

**CATALOGUE AND
MAIL ORDER**

CHAMBERS
P.O. Box 7841
San Francisco, CA 94120
800/334-9790
*(Bed linens and bedding
accessories)*

COLOGNE & COTTON
74 Regent Street
Leamington Spa
Warwickshire CV32 4NS
England
92/633-2573
(Classic bed linens)

THE COMPANY STORE
500 Company Store Road
La Crosse, WI 54601
800/323-8000 for catalogue
(Bed linens)

DOMESTICATIONS
P.O. Box 40
Hanover, PA 17333-0040
800/782-7722
(Discounted linens)

ELDRIDGE TEXTILE
COMPANY
277 Grand Street
New York, NY 10002
212/925-1523
*(Linens, comforters,
bedspreads, towels, rugs,
bathroom accessories)*

GARNET HILL
262 Main Street
Franconia, NH 03580
800/622-6216

REMO MAIL-ORDER
CATALOGUE
Oxford at Crown Street
Sydney, Australia
8/029-714
(Hip general store)

SEVENTH GENERATION
176 Battery Street
Burlington, VT 05401
802/658-7770 or
800/456-1177
*(Store with green products;
bed linens and bedding
accessories)*

**INTERNATIONAL
LISTINGS**

Canada

BRITISH COLUMBIA

MIRARI
576 Yates Street
Victoria V8W1K8
604/380-1114
(Bed linens)

QUEBEC

MARIE PAULE
1090 rue Laurier Ouest
Montreal
514/273-8889
(Bed linens)

OGILVY
1307 rue Sainte-Catherine
Ouest
Montreal
514/842-7711
(Bed linens and bedding)

France

PARIS

DESCAMPS
52, avenue Victor-Hugo
75116
45/00-70-22
(Bed linens)

INES DE LA
FRESSANGE
14, avenue Montaigne
75008
47/23-64-87
(Bed accessories)

SYBILLA
62, rue de Jean-Jacques
Rousseau
42/36-03-63
(Linens)

Great Britain

LONDON

THE ANTIQUE
TEXTILE CO.
100 Portland Road
W11
71/221-7730
(Bed linens)

THE CONRAN SHOP
Michelin House
81 Fulham Road
SW3
71/589-7401
(Bed linens, blankets, pillows,
duvet covers, and accessories)

THE GENERAL
TRADING COMPANY
144 Sloane Street
SW1
71/730-0411
(Bed linens)

GEORGE SPENCER
4 West Halkin Street
SW1
71/235-1501
(Classic English chintzes and
linens)

GIVAN'S IRISH LINEN
STORES LTD.
207 King's Road
SW3
71/352-6352
(Range of fine Irish bed
linens)

HABITAT
Heals Building
196 Tottenham Court Road
W1
71/631-3880

HARRODS
87-135 Brompton Road
Knightsbridge
SW1X 7XL
71/730-1234
(Wide range of quality linens)

HARVEY NICHOLS
Knightsbridge
SW1X 7RJ
71/235-5000

HEALS
196 Tottenham Court Road
W1
71/636-1666

THE IRISH LINEN CO.
35 Burlington Arcade
W1
71/493-8949
(Irish bed linens)

JOHN LEWIS
PARTNERSHIP
Oxford Street
W1
71/629-7711
(Wide range of all basic bed
linens)

LIBERTY
210-220 Regent Street
W1
71/734-1234
(Bed linens, with a wide range
of accessories)

LUNN ANTIQUES
86 New King's Road
SW6
71/736-4638
(Antique linens, bed covers, lace pillowcases and shams)

THE MONOGRAMMED
LINEN SHOP
168 Warton Street
SW3
71/589-4033
(Fine linens for bed and bath)

PETER JONES (BRANCH
OF JOHN LEWIS)
Sloane Square
SW1
71/730-3434
(Wide range of bedding needs)

SELFRIDGES
Oxford Street
W1
71/629-1234

BRYONY THOMASSON
283 Westbourne Grove
Portobello Road
W11
or by appointment
19 Ackmar Road
SW6
71/731-3693
(18th-century and 19th-century handwoven rustic textiles)

THE WHITE HOUSE
LINEN SPECIALIST
51 New Bond Street
W1
71/629-3521
(Classic bed linens)

Hong Kong

JOYCE INTIMATE
214B The Landmark
852/845-7665
(Bed linens)

Ireland

DUBLIN

BROWN, THOMAS & CO
LTD.
15-20 Grafton Street
2
1/679-5666

Italy

MILAN

BASSETTI
Corso Vercelli, 25
2/43-55-95
(Bassetti technique prints with contrasting prints on reverse side of sheets)

FRETTE
Via Manzoni, 11
2/86-43-39
(Classic luxury linens)

MIRABELLO
Via Montebello
(corner via S. Marco)
2/65-99-733
(Sheets, down-filled quilts)

PRATESI
Via Montenapoleone, 27E
2/76-01-27-55
(Luxury linens, bed covers)

VENICE

JESURUM
Ponte Canonica, 4310
41/5206-177
(Lace)

Japan

MUJIRUSHI SHOP
2-12-28 Kita Aoyama
Minato-ku
3/3478-5800
(Bed linens, curtains, household goods)

TAKASHIMAYA
4-4-1 Nihonbashi
Chuo-ku
3/3211-4111
(Bed linens and accessories)

RESOURCES

COVER FRONT

Antique **DUVET COVER** with button placket and inside duvet pocket - Anichini; "Loopy" standard **SHAM** by Angel Zimick - Portico Bed & Bath; Antique **EURO SHAMS** - The Vito Giallo Collection; **TOP SHEET** - Anichini; White polka dot "Mimosa" **BOTTOM SHEET** - Anichini; **DUVET** and feather bed - The Company Store

BACK

(on chair from top) Turkish **PILLOW-CASE** - Ad Hoc Softwares; blue **SHEET** - Ad Hoc Softwares; Buffalo plaid **BLANKET** and **TICKING PILLOW** - Paula Rubenstein; Denim **PILLOWCASE** - Ralph Lauren; Black and white plaid **BLANKET** - Ad Hoc Softwares; **CHAIR** - collection of Robert Valentine; (right of chair from top) Blue and white striped cotton **BLANKET** - Ad Hoc Softwares; red and white **TICKING PILLOW** - Paula Rubenstein; (behind chair) **IRON BED FRAME** and **CUSTOM MATTRESS** - ABC Carpet & Home; (on bed frame) Blue and white striped **MATTRESS TICKING** - Paula Rubenstein

BED LINENS

10 (from left) White goose down **COMFORTER** - The Company Store; Square **PILLOW** and **PILLOW COVER** - The Company Store; **NECK ROLL** in

Crespo Lino pillowcase - Anichini; (on stack from top) Blue **PILLOWCASE** - Ad Hoc Softwares; Blue and white striped **PILLOWCASE** - Ad Hoc Softwares; White with blue polka dot **PILLOWCASES** by Peter Reed for Design Guild - Portico Bed & Bath; Blue and white polka dot **PILLOW-CASES** by Peter Reed for Design Guild - Portico Bed & Bath; Blue and white striped **SHEET** - Anichini; White polka dot "Mimosa" **FITTED SHEET** - Anichini; Blue and white cotton "Amboise" **DUVET COVER** by Yves Delorme - Palais Royal; Blue **SHEET** - Anichini; Brahmsmount blue and white **COTTON BLANKET** - Portico Bed & Bath; White quilted C-103 **BED COVER** - Porthault; (on right) White **PILLOW** - The Company Store; Ticking **PILLOW** - Garnet Hill; Custom **MATTRESS** - ABC Carpet & Home; (behind) Custom-made upholstered **HEADBOARD** - ABC Carpet & Home

14 (from left) Jasmine boudoir **SHAM** - Terra Verde; Wool **THROW** - Ad Hoc Softwares; White lace **PILLOWCASE** - Fino Lino; Green cable **KNIT THROW** - Ad Hoc Softwares; Chenille **PILLOW-CASE** - Ad Hoc Softwares; (under) Matelassé **BEDSPREAD** - collection of Lynn Nigro, similar can be found at Wolfman • Gold & Good Co.

15 **MASSAGE OIL** by Aquamirabilis - Ad Hoc Softwares

16 **QUILT** by Judi Boisson - ABC Carpet & Home

18 SHEET - Bryony Thomasson, London;
BIRD'S NEST - collection of Maria
Robledo

0-21 (clockwise from upper left) *1)* BED SKIRT -
Palais Royal; **MATTRESS PAD** - The
Company Store; Quilted on top, fitted on
sides **MATTRESS, BOX SPRINGS,** and
FRAME - 1-800-Mattres *2)* Custom
MATTRESS PAD, MATTRESS, BOX SPRINGS -
1-800-Mattres; **BED SKIRT** "Echelle" dust
ruffle with border - Palais Royal *3)* **FITTED
SHEET** - Terra Verde; **PILLOWCASE** -
Wamsutta; **TATTOO** - Kaleidoscope;
PILLOW, PILLOW COVER - The Company
Store *4)* **TOP SHEET** with border - Palais
Royal; "Kashmir" 100 percent cashmere
BLANKET - Anichini; Quilted **BED
COVER** with scalloped edge - Porthault *5)*
100 percent **CASHMERE THROW** -
Anichini; C-20 **BED COVER** - Porthault;
"Echelle" **BED SKIRT** - Palais Royal *6)*
DUVET COVER - Palais Royal; "Regence"
COMFORTER - The Company Store; **BED
SKIRT** - Palais Royal; White with open cut
border, Palais Royal; **BED** - 1-800-Mattres;
PILLOWS - The Company Store *7)* White
diamond piqué **COVERLET** - Anichini;
BED SKIRT - Palais Royal; **BED** - 1-800-
Mattres *8)* **PILLOW** - The Company Store;
PILLOW PROTECTOR - The Company
Store; "Marina" **PILLOWCASE** with button
detail, Palais Royal; "Marina" beige **TOP
SHEET** by Yves Delorme - Palais Royal

22 Antique Fabric **TICKING PILLOW** and
BED ROLL - Paula Rubenstein; Blue and
white **TICKING PILLOW** - Garnet Hill

24 HOT WATER BOTTLE - drugstore;
Burkraft **WOOL THROW** - Ad Hoc
Softwares

25 FEATHER BED, PILLOW, PILLOW COVER -
The Company Store; Blue and white
SHEET - Anichini; **BED** - 1-800-Mattres

26 Camel and cream **TICKING PILLOW** -
Paula Rubenstein; **DOWN AND FEATHER**
- Mike's Down and Feather Shop

28 PILLOWS (from front) Antique **DREAM
PILLOW** - Anichini; **NECK ROLL** -
Wamsutta; "Sienne" **BOUDOIR PILLOW**
by Palais Royal - The Company Store;
Matelassé "Nevada" Boudoir **SHAM** by
Anichini - The Company Store; "Marina"
PILLOWCASE by Palais Royal - The
Company Store; "Good night kisses"
PILLOW by Angel Zimick - Joyce Boutique;
Patchwork **PILLOWCASE** by Angel Zimick
- Barneys; "Sienne" **EUROPEAN SQUARE**
by Palais Royal - The Company Store; (on
bed) **CASHMERE BLANKET** by Anichini -
The Company Store; "Sienne" **SHEET** by
Palais Royal - The Company Store

29 (from top) **PILLOW** - The Company
Store; **RECONDITIONED PILLOW** -
Mike's Down and Feather Shop; **TICKING
PILLOW** on bottom - Garnet Hill

30 PILLOW COVERS (from top) Striped
PILLOW with ties - ABC Carpet & Home;
"Marina" button **SHAM** - Palais Royal;
"Bellora" blue and white **EURO SHAM** -
Portico Bed & Bath; "Perles" **SHAM**
with scalloped edge - Palais Royal

32 **WHITE SHEET** - Wamsutta; **MATTRESS** - ABC Carpet & Home; **BOX SPRING** - 1-800-Mattres

34 **SHEET, DROP CLOTH** - Wamsutta

37 **COTTON BALL** - Mordern Artificial; **COTTON SHEET** - Wamsutta

38 Antique linen **TOP SHEET** - collection of Lynn Nigro; "Mimosa" polka dot **FITTED SHEET** - Anichini; **DUST RUFFLE** - Palais Royal at ABC Carpet & Home; **FEATHER BED** under fitted sheet - The Company Store; **BED** - 1-800-Mattres

39 **SHEET STRAPS** - F. W. Woolworth Co.; Wamsutta fitted **LINEN SHEET** - Portico Bed & Bath

40 **ANTIQUE LINENS** *Top shelf:* (from top) Guypere lace **PILLOWCASE** - E. Braun; Antique **PILLOWCASES** and European **SQUARE SHAMS** - The Vito Giallo Collection; *Middle shelf:* (left) **HEMP SHEETS** - Bryony Thomasson, London; (right) Red **CHECKERED FABRIC** - Bryony Thomasson, London; Antique lace **COMFORTER COVER** and Cluny lace **NECK ROLL** - Anichini; *Bottom shelf:* (left) **MATELASSÉ CLOTH** - The Vito Giallo Collection; (right) **TOP TOILE DE JOUY** - Bryony Thomasson; **MIDDLE TOILE DE JOUY** and **BOTTOM SHEET** - The Vito Giallo Collection; **SHELF UNIT** - Brian Windsor, Cynthia Beneduce Antiques

42 **BLENDED** color print sheets - Martex; **SOLID SHEETS** - Wamsutta; **WASHING MACHINE** - State Supply

43 **EUROPE'S CLASSICS** Yellow double line chain **SHEET** - Pratesi; Pink hearts **COTTON SHEET** - Porthault

44 **SPECIALTY SHEETS** (from left) **SATIN SHEET** - private collection; **FLANNEL SHEET** - L.L. Bean; **LATEX SHEET** - The Noose

45 **SATIN** (above, clockwise from upper left) "Cameillia" **PILLOW**, "Whisper" **PILLOW**, "Moonflowers" **BOUDOIR**, "Reverie" smocked **TOP SHEET** - all Cocoon; Green **BEDSPREAD** - Pratesi; "Shadow" **QUILT** - Cocoon; (below) "Reverie" smocked **TOP SHEET** - Cocoon; Green **BEDSPREAD** - Pratesi; "Shadow" **QUILT**, (on left) "Whisper" **PILLOW**, (on right) "Camellia" **PILLOW**, "Moonflowers" **BOUDOIR** - all Cocoon.

46 **SIMPLE SHEETS** - Wamsutta

BED COVERS

48 **BED COVER** Gray ivory king alpaca **BLANKET** - Anichini; White **SHEET** and **PILLOWCASES** - Wamsutta

50 Pendleton **BLANKET** - Paula Rubenstein

51 *(Top photo)* Chinchilla **BLANKETS,** Child's checked **BLANKET, SLEEPING BAGS** - Eastern Mountain Sports; *(Bottom photo)* Hudson Bay Point **BLANKETS**, six point with white stripes and four point white with candy stripes - L.L. Bean

52 **COMFORTER** - The Company Store; **COMFORTER COVER** by Peter Reed for Design Guild - Portico Bed & Bath; **MATTRESS** - custom-made; **TICK** Fabric - Waverly; **FUTON** and **BOX SPRINGS** covered with calf skin - collection of Lynn Nigro

54 Double wedding ring **QUILT** - Susan Parrish Antiques; **IRON BED** - ABC Carpet & Home; (in background) **QUILTED BED COVER** - Porthault

56 Louis Nichole chenille **COVERLET** - ABC Carpet & Home

IXING

58 **PILLOWCASES AND TOP SHEET** - Pratesi; "**AND**" **PILLOW** - Nina Ramsey Archipelago at Barney's; Black **MOHAIR BLANKET** - Palais Royal

60 **TOP SHEET, PILLOWCASES, NECK ROLLS** - Pratesi; "Zephyr" black and white tiny check **BOUDOIRS**, **EURO SHAMS** by Yves Delorme - Palais Royal; White **COVERLET** with scalloped edge - Anichini; Black **MOHAIR BLANKET** - Palais Royal

61 **TOP SHEET, STANDARD CASES, NECK ROLLS** - Pratesi; Burgundy **PILLOW-CASES** - Wamsutta; "Leonardo" **BED COVER** - Anichini; Black **MOHAIR BLANKET** - Palais Royal; Leopard **THROW** and **PILLOW** by Adrian Landau - ABC Carpet & Home; Leopard **BOLSTER** with tassel - ABC Carpet & Home; (in foreground) Red and white slipper **CHAIR** - collection of Robert Valentine

63 **LAYERING** "Vendange" - Pierre Frey for Palais Royal at ABC; **DUVET COVER** and **FITTED SHEET** - Wamsutta; India woven cotton **TOP SHEET**, solid **PILLOWCASE** and striped **PILLOWCASE** - Ad Hoc Softwares; **BED SKIRT** - Wamsutta; **TABLE** - ABC

64 **LAYERING** Mediterranean striped **TOP SHEET** and Merino Reale **BLANKET** - Garnet Hill; **BOTTOM SHEET** - Wamsutta; (on bed) Indonesian **THROW** and **SMALL PILLOW** - Boca Grande; Standard bed **PILLOW** - Paula Rubenstein; (over headboard) **THROW** - Boca Grande

65 **LAYERING** Blue and white hand-woven **PILLOWCASES** (large stripes)and **SHEET** from India - Ad Hoc Softwares; Turkish blue and natural (thin stripes) **PILLOWCASES** - Ad Hoc Softwares; **TICKING PILLOW** (on bottom) - Garnet Hill; Antique ticking **BOTTOM SHEET** - Paula Rubenstein; **BED SKIRT** - Palais Royal; **QUILT** - Judi Boisson for Garnet Hill

66 (in front) Large embroidered monogram **SHAM** and leaf border **SHAM** - The Vito Giallo Collection; White with blue polka dot **EMBROIDERY** - E. Braun; "Loopy" white **PILLOWCASE** with white looped fringe and "Veggie Dye" white **PILLOWCASE** with green ties both by Angel Zimick - Stanley Korshak, Dallas; Scalloped edge with coral **EMBROIDERY** and **MONOGRAM** - E. Braun.

67 **CONDOM PILLOW** by Angel Zimick - ABC; **TATTOO DESIGN** - Kaleidoscope; White **PILLOWCASE** - Wamsutta; **PILLOW** or **PILLOW PROTECTOR** - The Company Store

70 **ROMANTIC** Gold and orange **COMFORTER** - Frette; Paisley **BED-SPREAD** by Mulberry - ABC Carpet & Home; Leopard **THROW** and **PILLOW** by Adrian Landau - ABC Carpet & Home; **VELVET PILLOWS** - collection of Maria Robledo; Black **PILLOWS** - collection of Lynn Nigro; Leonardo Nuovo **COVERLET** in Bordeaux red - Anichini; Gold **SHEETS** of Egyptian cotton - Frette; (over bed board) Camel **THROW** made in Switzerland - Garnet Hill; **KILIM RUG** - ABC Carpet & Home; **BED** - collection of Maria Robledo

72 Antique **DUVET COVER** with button placket and inside duvet pocket - Anichini; "Loopy" standard **SHAM** by Angel Zimick - Portico Bed & Bath; Antique **EURO SHAMS** - The Vito Giallo Collection; **TOP SHEET** - Anichini; White polka dot "Mimosa" **BOTTOM SHEET** - Anichini; **DUVET** and **FEATHER BED** - The Company Store

73 Red and white **PILLOWS** - collection of Lynn Nigro; Toile de Jouy **PILLOW** with tassels - Rooms & Gardens; "Panier" **DUVET COVER** - Pierre Frey for Palais Royal at ABC Carpet & Home; Checked antique American **BED COVER** - Susan Parrish; Checked French **BED SKIRT** - Bryony Thomasson; fitted white **SHEET** - Wamsutta; Antique linen **TOP SHEET**

and small **PILLOW** - The Vito Giallo Collection; **FEATHER BED** - The Company Store

74 **RUGGED ROMANCE** Sheets - Bryony Thomasson, London; **BLANKET** - Portico Bed & Bath; Denim **PILLOWCASE** - Ralph Lauren; White **PILLOWCASE** - Wamsutta; Natural wool lift shearling **MATTRESS PAD** (used as throw at foot of bed) - Garnet Hill; **BED** - collection of Robert Valentine

75 (on chair from top) Turkish **PILLOW-CASE** - Ad Hoc Softwares; blue **SHEET** - Ad Hoc Softwares; Buffalo plaid **BLANKET** and **TICKING PILLOW** - Paula Rubenstein; Denim **PILLOWCASE** - Ralph Lauren; Black and white plaid **BLANKET** - Ad Hoc Softwares; **CHAIR** - collection of Robert Valentine; (left of chair from top) Blue and white striped cotton **BLANKET** - Ad Hoc Softwares; red and white **TICKING PILLOW** - Paula Rubenstein; (behind chair) **IRON BED FRAME** and **CUSTOM MATTRESS** - ABC Carpet & Home; (on bed frame) Blue and white striped **MATTRESS TICKING** - Paula Rubenstein

76 **STAGING** inspired by Matisse: **FUTON** and **BOX SPRINGS** covered with calf skin - private collection; Cream and gold **TICK PILLOWS** - Paula Rubenstein; Blue and white striped **FABRIC** - Paterson Silk; **TICKING PILLOWS** - Garnet Hill; Red and white antique **FABRIC** - Bryony Thomasson; **TICKING** on wall - Paula Rubenstein

78 **SIMPLE BED** White **SHEET** - Wamsutta; **TICKING PILLOWS** - Garnet Hill; Natural **DUVET** - The Company Store

U O T E S

2 **ANITA ENDREZZE,** "I Give You," *Yellow Silk* (Harmony Books, 1990).

8 **AUSTRALIAN ABORIGINAL SAYING**

11 **ENGLISH PROVERB,** *21st Century Dictionary of Quotations* (Dell Publishing, 1993).

13 **SOMERSET MAUGHAM,** *21st Century Dictionary of Quotations* (Dell Publishing, 1993).

19 **LEIGH HUNT,** *Correct Quotes* (WordStar International, 1992).

24 **EDITH WHARTON,** *Untamed Tongues: Wild Words from Wild Women* (Conari Press, 1993).

29 **DALAI LAMA,** *People* (September 10, 1979).

35 **DOROTHY PARKER,** *The Fifth and Far Finer than the First Four 637 Best Things Anybody Ever Said* (Ballantine Books, 1993).

47 **JOHN UPDIKE,** interview, 1993.

49 **FRAN LEBOWITZ,** *21st Century Dictionary of Quotations* (Dell Publishing, 1993).

55 **ROBERT HUGHES,** *Amish: The Art of the Quilt* (Alfred A. Knopf, 1993).

59 **PHYLLIS DILLER,** *Just Joking* (WordStar International, 1992).

72 **HENRY DAVID THOREAU,** *Correct Quotes,* (WordStar International, 1992).

75 **SIEGFRIED SASSOON,** *Bartlett's Familiar Quotations* (Little, Brown & Company, 1992).

76 **OSCAR WILDE,** *New York Times Book Review* (November 1993).

81 **WARNING,** *The 776 Stupidest Things Ever Said* (Mainstreet Books/Doubleday, 1993).

82 **QUENTIN CRISP,** *The Penguin Book of Modern Humorous Quotations* (Penguin Books, 1987).

83 **MARY WILSON LITTLE,** *An Uncommon Scold* (Simon & Schuster, 1989).

84 **HOW GIRLS CAN HELP THEIR COUNTRY,** *Girl Scout Manual,* 1913.

86 **KATHARINE HEPBURN,** *Vanity Fair* (January 1994).

104 **FRANK LLOYD WRIGHT,** *House Beautiful* (May 1993).

ACKNOWLEDGMENTS

MANUFACTURER & RETAIL RESEARCH
Jeannette Durkan

QUOTE RESEARCH
Lige Rushing & Kate Doyle Hooper

ORIGINAL INTERVIEWS
Cynthia Stuart

AND SPECIAL THANKS TO: Judy Aronowitz, Connie Bang, Amy Capen, Tony Chirico, M. Scott Cookson, Lauri Del Commune, Chris DiMaggio, Michael Drazen, Miki Duifterhof, Suzanne Eaton, Borden Elniff, Jane Friedman, Janice Goldklang, Meredith Harrington, Jo-Anne Harrison, Dina Dell'Arciprete-Houser, Patrick Higgins, Katherine Hourigan, Andy Hughes, Carol Janeway, Barbara Jones-Diggs, Nicholas Latimer, William Loverd, Anne McCormick, Dwyer McIntosh, Sonny Mehta, Lan Nguyen, Ingrid Nystrom, Kumiko Ohta, Janet Rouber, Suzanne Smith, Anne-Lise Spitzer, Meg Stebbins, Robin Swados, Aileen Tse, Rosa Villa, Shelley Wanger, Wayne Wolf.

COMMUNICATIONS

The world has gotten smaller and faster but we still can only be in one place at a time, which is why we are anxious to hear from you. We would like your input on stores and products that have impressed you. We are always happy to answer any questions you have about items in the book, and of course we are interested in feedback about Chic Simple.

Our address is:
84 WOOSTER STREET
NEW YORK, NY 10012
(212) 343-9677 • FAX (212) 343-9678
email address: **info@chicsimple.com**
compuserve number **72704,2346**

Stay in touch because
"The more you know, the less you need."

KIM JOHNSON GROSS & JEFF STONE

TYPE

The text of this book was set in two typefaces: New Baskerville and Futura. The ITC version of **NEW BASKERVILLE** is called Baskerville, which itself is a facsimile reproduction of types cast from molds made by John Baskerville (1706–1775) from his designs. Baskerville's original face was one of the forerunners of the typestyle known to printers as the "modern face"—a "modern" of the period A.D. 1800. **FUTURA** was produced in 1928 by Paul Renner (1878–1956), former director of the Munich School of Design, for the Bauer Type Foundry. Futura is simple in design and wonderfully restful in reading. It has been widely used in advertising because of its even, modern appearance in mass and its harmony with a great variety of other modern types.

SEPARATION AND FILM PREPARATION BY
APPLIED GRAPHICS TECHNOLOGIES
Carlstadt, New Jersey

PRINTED AND BOUND BY
FRIESEN PRINTERS
Altona, Manitoba, Canada

HARDWARE

Apple Macintosh Quadra 700 personal computers; APS Technologies Syquest Drives; Radius Precision Color Display/20; Radius 24X series Video Board; Hewlett Packard LaserJet 4, Supra Fax Modem

SOFTWARE

QuarkXPress 3.11, Adobe Photoshop 2.5.1, Microsoft Word 5.1, FileMaker Pro 2.0

MUSICWARE

The Breeders *(Last Splash)*; Radiohead *(Pablo Honey)*; Pearl Jam *(Pearl Jam)*; R.E.M. *(Reckoning)*; UB40 *(Promises and Lies)*; 10,000 Maniacs *(MTV Unplugged)*; Mazzy Star *(So Tonight That I Might See)*; Tina Turner *(Greatest Hits)*; Van Morrison *(Too Long in Exile)*; Duran Duran *(The Tour Sampler)*; Chris Isaak *(San Francisco Days)*; Steve Forbert *(The American in Me)*, Various Artists *(Alligator Stomp: Cajun & Zydeco Classics)*; Kate Bush *(The Whole Story)*; Lisa Stansfield *(Real Love)*; Various Artists *(Original Motion Picture Soundtrack of Singles)*; Lou Rawls *(The Legendary Lou Rawls)*

Special thanks to Cathy O'Brien of Capitol Records, Inc.

"A serene simplicity that is content with little, as long as that little is good."

FRANK LLOYD WRIGHT

professing his ideology